Hamlet Exposed!

A Shakespearean Comedy of
Elizabethan Errors

in One Act

By

George Freek

Published by

Blue Moon Plays

For That Once-In-A-Lifetime Blue Moon Experience

All rights reserved. Hamlet Exposed © George Freek 2022

All performances for any audience (classroom/auditorium/paying/nonpaying) must have applied for a performance license and paid performance fees in advance of production.

CAUTION: Professionals and amateurs are hereby warned that performance of *Hamlet Exposed* is subject to payment of a royalty unless written permission is given waiving such fee. The Play is fully protected under the copyright laws of the United States of America, and of all countries covered by the International Copyright Union (including the Dominion of Canada and the rest of the British Commonwealth), and of all countries covered by the Pan-American Copyright Convention, the Universal Copyright Convention, and the Berne Convention, and of all countries with which the United States has reciprocal copyright relations. All rights, including professional/amateur stage rights, motion picture, recitation, lecturing, public reading, radio broadcasting, television, video or sound recording, all other forms of mechanical or electronic reproduction, such as CD-ROM, CD-I, DVD, information storage and retrieval systems and photocopying, and the rights of translation into foreign languages, are strictly reserved. Particular emphasis is placed upon the matter of readings, permission for which must be secured from the Author in writing. Anyone receiving permission to produce the Play is required to give credit to the Author as sole and exclusive Author of the Play on the title page of all programs distributed in connection with performances of the Play and in all instances in which the title of the Play appears for purposes of advertising, publicizing or otherwise exploiting the Play and/or a production thereof. Author's name must be one-third the size of the title.

Digital versions cannot be added to a free or paid online library or website, in any format, with or without member access without the publisher's permission.

Publisher: Blue Moon Plays, LLC
1385 Fordham Road, Ste 105-279
Virginia Beach, VA 23464
Printed in the USA
ISBN # 978-1-943416-93-6
Editor Jean Klein
Cover Credit - George Cruikshank, Public domain, via Wikimedia Commons

CHANGES TO SCRIPT

Copyright law prevents this script from being copied or altered in any way by any technical or digital means. There may be no changes made to the script including but not limited to casting or dialogue without permission of the publisher and/or playwright.

PERFORMANCE/READING OF SCRIPT
This script is licensed for production by blue moon plays. It may NOT be performed or read aloud in any way (with or without admission fees) in a classroom, around a table, in front of a non-paying audience without a performance fee, which varies.

For any performance, you must apply for and purchase performance rights: in class, in school, for educational purposes, for paying or nonpaying audiences of any size, as a concert reading or a staged reading.

Anyone receiving permission to produce the Play is required to give credit to the Author as sole and exclusive Author of the Play on the title page of all programs distributed in connection with performances of the Play and in all instances in which the title of the Play appears for purposes of advertising, publicizing or otherwise exploiting the Play and/or a production thereof. Author's name must be one-half the size of the title.

All performances and/or readings of this script, whether or not admission fees are required, must apply for and receive a Performance License. There is a flat 100 fee if you wish to live stream performance.

Special Considerations:
Small-group readings around a table or in the classroom:
- If you are planning to use this script FOR CLASSROOM USE, you must purchase scripts for the members of your class or group. These may be purchased as a downloadable PDF (class/group study pack) which may be printed for that class only.
- If you are a small group doing private play readings for YOUR OWN ENTERTAINMENT or for a SMALL SENIOR ACTIVITY GROUP, you must purchase the number or scripts

required by the characters: these may be purchased as a multi-copy download which will give you a printable script that you may copy for that reading only.

Video Taping
One video tape may be made for archival purposes only.

Livestreaming
Livestreaming is permissible with an additional fee.

Digital versions cannot be added to a free or paid online library or website, in any format, with or without member access, without the publisher's permission.

For information, visit www.havescripts.com;
email info@bluemoonplays.com
or call 757-816-1164

TO PERFORM THIS PLAY

You must buy sufficient scripts for the cast + 3, apply for performance rights, pay the performance fee, and receive a performance license.

To purchase scripts:

- Purchase sufficient printed hard copies (one for each cast member, plus 3 for the crew) - an automatic 10 percent discount is applied to multiple printed hardcopies at the point of ordering.
or
- Purchase a Multicopy PDF which allows you to print sufficient copies of this script (one for each cast member, plus 3 for the crew). Click Return to Merchant to download your printable PDF. A link to the download will also be emailed to you, along with a link to the application for performance license.

To apply for a Performance License, go to the Product Page of the play and fill out and submit the application form.

To pay the Performance Fee, simply pay the invoice you will be emailed when we receive your application for performance.

Your Performance License for your requested dates will be emailed to you.

All scripts and licenses shall be obtained at Blue Moon Plays at www.havescripts.com

If you wish to make changes in the script of any kind, you must receive permission from the publisher or the playwright. Permission is usually granted readily when schools or theaters face casting problems and the changes do not affect the quality or intent of the original.

Hamlet Exposed!

THE CHARACTERS

GERTRUDE, Hamlet's mother, the Queen, 40s

CLAUDIUS, The King and Hamlet's father-in-law, also his uncle, 40s

HAMLET, The Prince, 21

HORATIA, Hamlet's childhood friend, 20

OPHELIA, A beautiful young woman, in love with Laertes, 19

POLONIUS, Ophelia's father, the court chirurgeon, 50

LAERTES, Polonius's adopted son, in love with Ophelia, 21

THE PLACE

Elsinore Castle

An empty stage

Hamlet Exposed!

(*At rise: A bare stage. GERTRUDE and CLAUDIUS are engaged in conversation*)

CLAUDIUS: My dear, at any time your Hamlet will be here with us.

GERTRUDE (*Worried*): I am surprised it took him so long to return to us.

CLAUDIUS: Well, Gertrude, Wittenberg is far away, and he was so close to finishing his studies he must have decided to stay and complete them. After all, what good for him if he came home prematurely?

GERTRUDE: He might have wanted to comfort his mother in her grief!

CLAUDIUS: Perhaps he felt I could do that.

GERTRUDE: Oh, I'm sorry, my dear. Of course you can. I fear you think I baby Hamlet. Admit it.

CLAUDIUS: All right, I admit it.

GERTRUDE (*Shocked*): You really do!

CLAUDIUS: Gertrude, you must face the fact. Hamlet is a child no longer. And now that his father is dead, he must become a man—

GERTRUDE (*Cutting him off, strained*): Yes, and when he comes home that will happen… My Love…

CLAUDIUS (*Mildly disturbed*): I only hope all goes well.

GERTRUDE: But why should it not?

CLAUDIUS: My dear, you must admit that Hamlet was very close to his father.

GERTRUDE: Oh, I certainly do admit it. After all, his father spoiled him almost to rottenness! He indulged his each and every whim. He gave him all he asked for and prepared Hamlet for kingship in his own image. That is, teaching him to drink like a fish, to chase loose women and to treat all others as if they were his footstools.

CLAUDIUS (*Uneasily*): And I fear Hamlet adored him for it.

GERTRUDE: But he will soon be home, and his brute of a father is dead. So finally I can tell him the truth about… that man.

CLAUDIUS: Are you certain that be wise? The truth is often hard to hear. That is why 'tis 'bitter.

GERTRUDE: I am certain!

CLAUDIUS (*Slightly pontifical*): But remember this, my dear, as grows the tree, so grows the limb, and as Aristotle tells us 'The apple falleth not far from the tree.'

GERTRUDE: Oh, piffle! Hamlet must hear the truth!

CLAUDIUS: But will he believe you?

GERTRUDE: I'm his mother!

CLAUDIUS: 'Tis true, a man's mother is his mother, while his father is a matter of opinion—

GERTRUDE: What! Claudius!

CLAUDIUS: I only hope Hamlet doesn't resent me.

GERRRUDE: Resent *you*! But he has always liked you.

CLAUDIUS: Yes, but as an uncle, not as a stepfather.

GERTRUDE: But Hamlet is kind and he is gentle. He will certainly recognize the truth when he hears it.

CLAUDIUS: Perhaps… But be gentle with him, my dear. Remember that Hamlet has suffered a great blow. The sudden death of a father is like a sudden storm upon on a calm sea—

GERTRUDE: Yes, yes… of course I'll be gentle. Oh, Claudius, darling, you are so kind, so good… (She suddenly embraces him, as…)

(HAMLET *then enters. He smirks knowingly, seeing them embrace*)

HAMLET: Ahem.

GERTRUDE: Hamlet! My darling! You are home at last! (She embraces him).

HAMLET: Hello, mother dear. (Raised eyebrow) I hope you are well.

GERTRUDE: I am, now that you are here.

CLAUDIUS (With avuncular good nature): Hello, Hamlet, my boy!

HAMLET: Hello…Uncle Claudius. (They also embrace).

GERTRUDE: But now you must call him father, Hamlet.

HAMLET: Call him Father Hamlet?

CLAUDIUS: Tut, tut, Gertrude, you must let him get used to the fact! And try to remember Hamlet, my boy, that time heals all wounds, for time and tide waiteth for no—

HAMLET: (*Cutting him off, ironically*): But perhaps I should say… 'My King'?

CLAUDIUS: Hamlet… my son, if only in spirit… know that this crown sits on my head only until you are deemed worthy to wear it yourself. I am as it were, merely your stand-in, until the Elder Councilors declare you fit to rule. At that time, I will happily place it upon your noble brow with the utmost—

HAMLET: Yes, I'm sure I am indebted to you… uncle.

GERTRUDE: But for the moment forget all that. Hamlet, there is much I have to tell you—

HAMLET (*Archly*): Is there? You mean about my father's death?

GERTRUDE: That, among other things… about your father—

(*Then HORATIA suddenly enters, excited to see HAMLET once again*)

HERATIA: Hamlet! Then 'tis true you've returned!

HAMLET: Loyal Horatia! (They embrace)

HORATIA: How glad I am to see you!

HAMLET *(Meaningfully)*: And I'm sure you have many, many things to tell me.

HORATIA" Oh boy, do I *not*! You would not believe whom Rinaldo up and married... old blubber lips! And Bertolo, I am almost ashamed to tell you—

CLAUDIUS (*Chuckling, To GERTRUDE*): My dear, why do we not allow these young people to renew their friendship, whilst we prepare for a feast in honor of young Hamlet's return?

GERTRUDE: Yes that is fitting. (*To HAMLET*) But my dear, there are things you must know... and the sooner the better! (She and CLAUDIUS exit).

HORATIA: It's wonderful to see you looking so well. I haven't played tennis in I don't know how long! But how have you kept?

HAMLET (*Walking away*): Oh Horatia, that this too, too solid flesh would melt away—

HORATIA: *What*! Hamlet, are you ill!

HAMLET: Not of any specific illness, Horatia. But I tell you now... Something is rotten in the state of Denmark!

HORATIA: It's not me!

HAMLET: Oh, Horatia… do you not find it strange that Claudius is King?

HORATIA: No.

HAMLET (*Pre-occupied*): Yes, of course… And that is because… (*He stares at her*) You *don't*?

HORATIA: Should I?

HAMLET: Well, was not my father King?

HORATIA: He was.

HAMLET: And am I not the King's *son*?

HORATIA: You are.

HAMLET: Well then…

HAMLET: And your mother the Queen married your Uncle Claudius, who was the younger son of the older King, your grandfather, and therefore—

HAMLET: No! That is not the way it should work! When King dies, King's son becomes new King! Now do you get it, numbskull!

HORATIA: Numbskull!

HAMLET: Oh, I'm sorry, Horatia. I am… distracted.

HORATIA: But Hamlet, you *will* be King.

HAMLET: Ha! Think you so?

HORATIA: Of course! When our wise Council of Elders deems—

HAMLET (*Scoffs*): And believe you that... bull twaddle?

HORATIA: Do you not?

HAMLET: Oh, Horatia, Horatia! Listen to me. What if I were to tell you that my father, the King... (*He thinks*)... was *murdered*?

HORATIA: But why would you tell me that?

HAMLET: Because, numb because... *Sweet* Horatia... It is true!

HORATIA: Who told you this, Hamlet!

HAMLET (*Thinks, pacing*): Well, he himself did!

HORATIA: He! You mean... your father? (*He nods*) But... is he not dead? And if he is dead how could he tell you he was murdered? And if he could tell you he was murdered, then... He must not be dead! (Shakes her head) I don't get it.

HAMLET (*Fumbling*): It was not he... exactly. It was... his *ghost*. Yes, his ghost told me.

HORATIA: His ghost! Whoa! Methinks you are too much in the sun, Hamlet! I know you have had a great shock, but—

HAMLET: It was, blast you... in a dream! In a dream his ghost told me so!

HORATIA: Oh. But Hamlet can we believe in dreams! Sometimes I know that dreams may portend the future, but events in the *past*? Why, I myself saw your father killed by Fortinbras of Norway in a fair fight.

HAMLET: That is what you believed you saw, Horatia. But just before that fight he was… poisoned, to make it appear *as if* he were killed in the fight!

HORATIA: (*Very skeptically*) *Poisoned*?

HAMLET: 'Sblood, Horatia! I have it from his very lips!

HORATIA: (*Still skeptical*) Well Yesss, but… in a dream…

HORATIA: You doubt my word! My dearest friend! Shall I swear it… On a <u>Bible</u>? All right, where is a <u>Bible</u>… *(He makes a pretense of searching for a Bible)*…

HORATIA (*Shaking her head*): I don't wish to doubt, Hamlet, but this story amazes me!

HAMLET: There are stranger things in heaven and earth, Horatia, than your philosophy ever dreamed of!

HORATIA: I've heard that. But Hamlet… what do you intend to do about it?

HAMLET: Aye, there's the rub. For the moment I think it best if I play the 'Melancholy Prince' in order to gain time.

HORATIA (*Uneasy*): Time… for what?

HAMLET: That is where your help is needed. Here is what you must do. You must spread this murder story among the citizens, so that when I make my play I will have the support of the rabble—

HORATIA: The *rabble*!

HAMLET: I meant… the people…

(*Then CLAUDIUS re-enters. HAMLET, seeing him, immediately turns 'melancholy'*)

CLAUDIUS: The feast is being prepared. The cook says we are to have funeral-baked meats. I hope they are not too spoiled!

HAMLET (*As if distraced*): A Feast, a feast, a feast! And what is a feast!

CLAUDIUS (*Alarmed, to HORATIA*): What's this?

HORATIA (*Scratching her head*): I know not, My Lord.

HAMLET (*Whispers to HORATIA, as he passes by her*): Melancholy, numbskull…

HORATIA: I know not, but I fear Hamlet is… melancholy.

CLAUDIUS: Oh no! Gentle Hamlet… are you melancholy?

HAMLET: Oh, My Lord, I could be enclosed in a nutshell and consider myself a King of Infinite Space if I did not have… bad dreams…

HORATIA: My Lord! He said the very same to me!

CLAUDIUS (*Highly alarmed*): This is not a good thing!

HAMLET (*Appears to be near tears*): I have lost all sense of happiness. My mood is so heavy that this lovely dwelling, this earth seems to me like nothing but a barren rock! What a piece of work is man, how noble in proportion, and yet to me what is this but perfection of dust! No man giveth me delight and neither doth any woman.

GERTRUDE (*Entering, is ghast*) What's this! Not thy Mother!

HORATIA: Not thy *dearest* friend!

HAMLET: Away! Get thee to a nunnery! (*He exits*)

CLAUDIUS (*Shaking his head, watching HAMLET exit*): I'm worried about that boy!

GERTRUDE: Oh, Horatia! Know you something of this?

HORATIA (*Very uneasy*): Methinks it has somewhat to do with his father's death.

CLAUDIUS: Yes, methought so.

GERTRUDE: But what are we to do!

CLAUDIUS: I will think on it. And in the meantime, Horatia, follow him. Do not let him do anything rash.

HORATIA: I will do't, My Lord. (*She exits*)

GERTRUDE: Claudius, he is so melancholy! What are we to do?

CLAUDIUS: I am still thinking.

GERTRUDE: Well, hurry up and think!

CLAUDIUS: I think…

GERTRUDE: Yes, yes…

CLAUDIUS: I think… that Polonius should speak to him.

GERTRUDE: Of course! Polonius, the court chirurgeon…

CLAUDIUS: He is wise and subtle in the workings of the mind.

GERTRUDE: Yes! He'll know what is to be done! Let's us get him at once! (*They exit*)

(*As they exit left, OPHELIA and LAETRES then enter from the right*)

LAERTES: So then, My Sweet Ophelia, all is settled between you and I?

OPHELIA: 'Tis Laertes.

LAERTES: But your father…

OPHELIA: 'Tis his wish also.

LAERTES: 'Tis? Then am I the most fortunate man on this planet!

OPHELIA: And certain of your love, Laertes, I am the most fortunate woman!

LAERTES: But there is one thing, which worries me.

OPHELIA: What is that?

LAERTES: Know you that Prince Hamlet has returned from Wittenberg?

OPHELIA: What of it?

LAERTES: Well… I know that he professes… some feelings for you.

OPHELIA: Ugh!

HAMLET: Then you care not for him?

OPHELIA: That *toad*! Maketh me not to laugh. (*She laughs*).

LAERTES: Then I am assured?

OPHELIA: You are, silly Laertes.

LAERTES: Then I am the most happy—

OPHELIA: I know! I know! But why do you not go and speak to my father?

LAERTES (*He gulps*): Now?

OPHELIA (*Caressing him*): What better time to strike than while… the *iron* is hot?

LAERTES (*Screwing up his courage*): I'll do't. But Sweet Ophelia, before I do, may I beg one favor of you…

OPHELIA (*Kisses him*): Do you have it?

LAERTES (*Ecstatically*): Vavavoom! *(He rushes off)*

(And as LAERTES exits to the left, HAMLET once more enters from the right)

HAMLET: Ophelia… Oho, this is well met…

OPHELIA (*Irked but polite*): How goes it, My Lord?

HAMLET; Ophelia, I… would like *to be*…

HAMLET: What would you like to be, My Lord?

HAMLET: I'd like to be your Lord… and your Master! (*He then tries to kiss her*).

OPHELIA: Fie, my Lord! What is this? I will believe you do not respect me!

HAMLET: Oh, I will gladly show you—

OPHELIA: What will you gladly show me, My Lord? No! Striketh that!

HAMLET: Why, I will gladly show you how *much* I respect you! (*He again grabs her*).

OPHELIA (*Pushing him away*): My Lord, this is too much!

HAMLET: Methinks it's not enough! (*He tries again*)

OPHELIA: Hamlet, you are rude!

HAMLET: Ha! But methinks you will sing a different tune... when I am King!

OPHELIA: When will that be?

HAMLETL (*Slyly*): Sooner than you think, Sweet Ophelia, sooner than you think!

OPHELIA: My Lord, I think you are suddenly... not so melancholy!

HAMLET: Melancholy! Yes... melancholy! Oh, but I am... (*Assumes a melancholy pose*) I am a very melancholy Prince, Ophelia. (*He then exits*).

(*And as HAMLET exits right, POLONIUS then enters from the left*)

POLONIUS: Ophelia, my dear one...

OPHELIA: Hello, father.

POLONIUS: Can it be true?

OPHELIA: Mean you Hamlet's rudeness? Yes, but he has always been a nerd! And if he *does* become King, I truly fear for our country—

POLONIUS: I mean what Laertes just told me!

OPHELIA (*Rapturously*): Oh! Yes, 'tis true. Laertes and I are in love and we ask only for your blessing before we plight our troth!

POLONIUS: My Dear! You have made me the happiest father in Christendom! Know you this has been my fondest desire since Laertes' father and mother were killed in the Norwegian raids of '63, and we brought him as a tiny lad into our household!

OPHELIA: And it has been my desire also, father.

POLONIUS: He is a young man of outstanding character! He is brave, yet courteous, strong, yet gentle, kind, but firm. And also his bones and sinews, heart and lungs are in excellent health! (*He chuckles*) Oh yes, Laertes is good breeding stock, Ophelia, and if you will bless me thricefold, you will give me wise and healthy grandchildren! And first of all healthy, because if we have not our health, then we have not—

OPHELIA: Yes, yes… now I will go find Laertes, and tell him the news. (*She exits*).

POLONIUS: Do't, My Dear.

(*And while OPHELIA is exiting right, CLAUDIUS and GERTRUDE enter left*)

CLAUDIUS: Polonius, Good Polonius! Heaven be praised we have found you!

POLONIUS: What's this! Claudius and Gertrude, My Queen… Did you think I was lost?

CLAUDIUS: No, 'tis Hamlet!

POLONIUS: Hamlet is lost?

CLAUDIUS: No, *no* Good Polonius! know you that our son, Prince Hamlet is returned from Wittenberg?

POLONIUS (*Confused*): And he's lost?

GERTRUDE: Aye, in hs mind! We fear something is disturbing him!

POLONIUS: What is it?

CLAUDIUS (*With a galnce at GERTRUDE*): Concerning his father's death, I fear.

POLONIUS: And what of his father's death is disturbing him?

CLAUDIUS: Why, the fact of it!

GERTRUDE: Oh, good Polonius, Hamlet is… *melancholy*!

POLONIUS: No!

CLAUDIUS: Yes!

POLONIUS: Hm… (*He thinks deeply*) The cause of Melancholy, My Lord, is often a surfeit of black bile, which then engorges the liver ducts. Know you if Hamlet has ingested an excess of black bile recently?

CLAUDIUS: How would we know that?

POLONIUS: Why, he might have taken excessive eel intestines or he might have—

GERTRUDE: But Claudius, how in Heaven's name can we know what he has taken, since he has only recently returned from Wittenberg!

CLAUDIUS (*Nodding sagely*): 'Tis true.

GERTRUDE: Good Polonius, cannot you speak with him and by clever means root out this melancholy?

POLONIUS: I can! I'll do't, My Queen.

GERTRUDE: Oh, thank you, Good Polonius, oh, thank you!

CLAUDIUS: And if you succeed, we will owe you much.

POLONIUS: I'll do't not for gain, My Lord, but to please my King and Queen. And remember Melancholy is not so harmful as you may think. Why, 'tis often nothing more than a superabundance of Phlegm or an imbalance between the black and yellow bile, which when out of balance may cause the stomach to engorge and cause an eruption in the—

GERTRUDE (*Nnauseated*): Yes, yes… we are certain you know best… Good Polonius.

POLONIUS: But where will I find Prince Hamlet, if he is lost?

CLAUDIUS (*Pointing*): Is not that he?

(*HAMLET then enters. He appears to be very melancholy*)

POLONIUS: So 'tis.

GERTRUDE (*Nearly in tears*): Oh, see how melancholy he is!

Polonius: He does seem so. And now, My Lord, 'tis best methinks if Hamlet and I were left alone. Leave him to my care.

CLAUDIUS: Come, Gertrude. Let us leave the chirurgeon to his work.

GERTRUDE: And I will pray for your success, Good Polnius. *(They exit)*.

CLAUDIUS (*Slowly approaches HAMLET*): Prince Hamlet, A good day to you, My Lord…

Hamlet (Melancholy): No! 'Tis not a good day, sir.

POLONIUS: Sir? But Hamlet, do not you know me?

HAMLET *(He peers at him):* Yes, I think that I do…

POLONIUS: Of course you do. Who am I?

HAMLET: Do *you* not know?

POLONIUS (*Irked*): Of course *I* know!

HAMLET: Hm… Methinks you are a fishmonger.

POLONIUS: *I*! A fishmonger!

HAMLET: Yes! You are a fishmonger.

POLONIUS: Hm… (*To himself*) Is there a method in his melancholy? (*To HAMLET*) I fear you mistake me, My Lord.

HAMLET: What did you say that I mistook you?

POLONIUS: That I was a fishmonger.

HAMLET: *You* said that you were a fishmonger?

POLONIUS: No! *I* did not!

HAMLET: But then how did I mistake you?

POLONIUS (*Growing angry*): *You* said I was a fishmonger! You mistook me for a fishmonger!

HAMLET: And still I say it. You are a fishmonger.

POLONIUS: No, My Lord, I am not!

HAMLET: Oh yes, my fishmonger, you are.

POLONIUS (*Stamping his foot*): I am *not*!

HAMLET: You are.

POLONIUS: Not!

HAMLET: Are!

POLONIUS: My Lord! *You* are insolent! (*Angrily he turns his back to HAMLET*)

HAMLET: My Good Sir, *you* are a fishmonger. (*He kicks POLONIUS in the pants*).

POLONIUS: My Lord! I dare you to do that again! Oops! *(He turns and rushes off)*

HAMLET: Oho! (*As POLONIUS rushes off, HAMLET laughingly kicks him again*).

POLONIUS (*Running off*): Ouch! Insolence, cruel insolence!

HAMLET: Haha! These fools to me are as flies to wanton boys! I *kick* them for my sport!

(And now Ophelia enters. She has just witnessed HAMLET's attack on POLONIUS)

OPHELIA: Fie, My Lord! Are not you ashamed?

HAMLET: Sweet Ophelia! Will you give me something?

OPHELIA (*wary*): What is it?

HAMLET (*He leers*): Something to be *truly* ashamed of!

OPHELIA: Fie again, My Lord! And tell me. Do you attack only gray-haired old men!

HAMLET: No, I do not.

OPHELIA: You do! I just saw you!

HAMLET: But not *only* gray-haired old men. I also attack fair-haired young women! (*He grabs at her*)

OPHELIA: My Lord, can this rudeness be!

HAMLET: Oh yes, it can, Sweet Ophelia, yes, it can! (*He chases her off*)

(*And as Ophelia runs off left, HORATIA enters from the right, stopping HAMLET*)

HORATIA: My Lord! Know you that Ophelia is betrothed to Laertes?

HAMLET: Horatia! We are well met! Now tell me… How goes our plot?

HORATIA (*Uneasy*): Well, My Lord, I have spread your story of poison and murder among the kitchen staff—

HAMLET: 'Tis good, Horatia, 'tis very good!

HORATIA: And in secret I have told it to the castle churls…

HAMLET: That's it, Horatia! You have done your job well!

HORATIA (*Gloomily*): I have done my best, My Lord.

HAMLET: Then, Horatia, have no fear! Our time draws near! (*He suddenly begins to soliloquize*) 'To be or not to be, that is the question—'

HORATIA: Not yet, My Lord…

HAMLET: Not yet?

HORATIA: Methinks not.

HAMLET (*Somewhat piqued*): Why not?

HORATIA: I see Laertes coming toward us, and he seemeth incensed.

HAMLET: Piffle! Laertes is a jackass.

HORATIA: But methinks an angry jackass is not to be trifled with.

(*Then LAERTES storms onto the stage carrying a glove. He comes up to HORATIA*)

LAERTES (*He looks HAMLET up and down*): Are *you* My Lord Hamlet?

(Insulted) What's this? Know me not?

LAERTES: I thought that I knew Lord Hamlet. I thought I knew him to be the Prince of
Denmark.

HAMLET: So I am!

LAERTES: But I have heard that this so-called *Prince* Hamlet behaves not like a Prince at all, but more like a Prince's… fishmonger.

HAMLET: Fishmonger! You are insolent, Laertes!

LAERTES: Well, know that if you be Hamlet…

HAMLET: I *am* he!

LAERTES: Then you are not a Prince, but a boorish churl! (*He slaps him with the glove*)

HAMLET: Ouch! That hurt!

LAERTES: That is for insulting Good Polonius!

HAMLET: Do that again!

LAERTES (*He slaps HAMLET again*): That is for insulting my betrothed!

HAMLET: What! You're betrothed to *Polonius*?

LAERTES: To Ophelia! (*He thinks, slaps him again*) And that is for insulting *me*!

HORATIA: Gentlemen, I pray you enough of this—

HAMLET: Stand back Horatia! This is intolerable!

LAERTES: So you will not tolerate it?

HAMLET: I will not!

LAERTES: Then, My Lord, you must seek satisfaction.

HORATIA (*Tugging furiously at HAMLET's sleeve*): My Lord, a word…

HAMLET (*To HORATIA*): Away! (*To LAERTES*) I'll do't, man!

LAERTES: Then I will be here tomorrow… at eleven bells!

HAMLET: I cannot waiteth! Why, I shall slice off your—

LAERTES: And ask not for whom eleven bells toll Prince Hamlet! Ask not! (*He exits*)

HORATIA (*Greatly distressed*): Oh, My Lord…

LAERTES: Horatia, did you see the nerve of the churl!

HORATIA: Yes, I did. But perhaps you were rash.

HAMLET: Rash! Ha, I will slice him into titbits for the castle dogs!

HORATIA: My Lord… knew you Yorick?

HAMLET: Ah, Yorick! Why, he is the greatest fencer in all of Denmark!

HORATIA: The finest fencer, save one… Yorick was killed, My Lord.

HAMLET: What! Yorick killed! Alas, poor Yorick, I knew him well, Horatia.

HORATIA: He was killed, My Lord, by Laertes.

HAMLET: Laertes! Mean you… *this* Laertes!

HORATIA: The very one.

HAMLET: 'Sblood! But then, Horatia, we must hurry our plan, for if tomorrow at eleven tolls of the bell I am King, then Laertes can do nothing! Why, I might have him declared outlaw or traitor to his King!

HORATIA: Um, about the plan, My Lord…

HAMLET: I know, I know, we must work fast! But if we screw our purpose to the stars—

HORATIA: My Lord, we have a problem…

HAMLET: A problem? What is it?

HORATIA: I told the castle peasants, My Lord. I spread your story of poison among the people—

HAMLET: Yes, yes… and they responded to't, did they not?

HORATIA: They did, My Lord. They responded… by laughing in my face!

HAMLET: What! Laughing!

HORATIA: And also by threatening to have me drawn and quartered as a traitor!

HAMLET: Surely not, Horatia!

HORATIA: Surely so, My Lord!

HAMLET: Why, those nincompoops, that filthy rabble! Oh, what a silly piece of work is man, Horatia, how disgusting in design, how lowly in mind—

HORATIA: I swear I did my duty to you, My Lord. I am sorry I failed.

HAMLET: But then we have no hope from this scum! And there is truly… no hope?

HORATIA (*Hangs her head*): I fear not.

HAMLET (*He gulps*): And so tomorrow and tomorrow… I truly hopeth there is… a tomorrow creeps into this petty pace, from day to day—

HORATIA: Yes, My Lord, but tomorrow… at eleven bells…

HAMLET: I know, I know! And yet… I am a fine fencer, Horatia.

HORATIA: You are that, My Lord.

HAMLET: Why, I might win…

HORATIA (*Failing to stifle her sobs*): Yes, you might…

HAMLET: In a fair fight… (*Brainstorm*) Aha! But Horatia, who says't must be a *fair* fight!

HORATIA (Sadly): The judges say it, My Lord.

HAMLET: Oh yes… the judges…

HORATIA (*Starts to cry again*): Oh My Good… Hamlet…

HAMLET: Desist!

HORATIA: I'm sorry, My Lord… but, while there is yet time, I wish to… make you aware of some thing…

HORATIA: I believe I am aware of 't, Sweet Horatia.

HORATIA: Then you know… that I…

HAMLET: And I… I also… like you *very much*, Horatia.

HORATIA: Oh, My Lord… (*She wails again*).

HAMLET (*He walks off, starts to soliloquize*): 'To be or not to be, that is the question'—

HORATIA: Not yet, My Lord…

HAMLET (*Irate*): Why the devil not!

HORATIA: Look you there.

(*And then CLAUDIUS and GERTRUDE enter. However, they are pre-occupied*)

GERTRUDE: Oh, this is dreadful news, Claudius!

CLAUDIUS: 'Tis, My Queen! 'Tis most unfortunate. (*Orating*) And yet, at the most treacherous of times, My Dear, we oft find within ourselves the power and, thus the means, whether by hook or by crook, to meet the challenge, to face the adversity, and by facing it to conquer it—

GERTRUDE (*Exasperated*): Yes, yes, Claudius… but *how*!

CLAUDIUS (*Sighs*): I know not.

GERTRUDE: Cannot we send an ambassador to Fortinbras to stall for time?

CLAUDIUS: Yes, we could do that.

GERTRUDE: Someone who might justly argue in our cause and, by powers of persuasion, even, perchance to convince him to desist in his intention to invade our borders?

CLAUDIUS: I myself would gladly do't, but 'tis not seemly for a King—

GERTRUDE: Oh yes, 'tis beneath your dignity, My Lord.

(*Ovehearing them, HAMLET and HORATIA now step forward inquisitively*)

HAMLET: What is't, Mother? You are greatly disturbed.

GERTRUDE: Greatly…

CLAUDIUS: Good Prince, we have just received word that Fortinbras of Norway, hot upon the killing of your father, intends to push his ill-gotten victory unto the bosom of our fair Denmark!

HORATIA: An invasion!

HAMLET: 'Tis an outrageous insult!

CLAUDIUS: We are in need of an ambassador! Someone with great powers of persuasion…

HORATIA (*A light dawning*): An ambassador with powers of persuasion…

CLAUDIUS: With consummate skill in disputation…

HORATIA (*The brainstorm*): Don't they learn disputation at *Wittenberg*! (*HAMLET surreptitiously kicks her*).

CLAUDIUS: And someone who may speak with the authority and force of Denmark backing him—

HORATIA: My Lord!

GERTRUDE (*Looking at HORATIA, getting it*): Why, of course! Hamlet!

HAMLET: Yes, mother?

GERTRUDE: We must send *you*, Hamlet!

CLAUDIUS: But my dear… Hamlet is melancholy.

HORATIA: But he is not!

HAMLET: I am not?

HORATIA (*Aside, to HAMLET*): Think you of Laertes, My Lord! (*To GERTRUDE*) My Queen, he has been cured of his melancholy!

GERTRUDE: Can this be true! Hamlet, are you truly cured of your melancholy?

HORATIA: Aye, he is! (*Quickly, to HAMLET*) And now have you opportunity to confront the *true* killer of your father, Hamlet! 'Tis just what the chirurgeon ordered!

CLAUDIUS: Well then, 'tis settled!

GERTRUDE: Oh, Hamlet, although I did wish to speak to you of certain matters—

CLAUDIUS: There is no time, Gertrude.

Well, my son, I will say only this. Your father did spoileth you unto rottenness—

CLAUDIUS: And so come, Gertrude. We must prepare for his departure at once. And Hamlet, let me advise you… neither borrower nor lender be for loan oft loses both itself and friend—

GERTRUDE (*A bit short*): There is no time, Claudius. (*Hauling CLAUDIUS off*) God's speed, dear son. (*They are gone*).

The devil taketh me! Horatia, must I do't?

HORATIA: Why Hamlet, 'tis for your country!

HAMLET: I am in great confusion! (*Pause*) 'To be or not to be, that is the question'—

HORATIA: My Lord, *not now*!

HAMLET *(He stamps his foot angrily)*: Why not!

HORATIA: Because, My Lord, 'Tis time for us to make haste to Norway! *(She then starts to pull him away)*

HAMLET (*Shakes free*): No! Horatia! I'll do't! (*She looks impatiently on as once again he begins to soliloquize*) 'To be or not to be, that is the question. Whether 'tis nobler in the mind to suffer the slings and arrows of outrageous forune or to take arms against a sea of troubles and by opposing'—

(The lights suddenly begin to fade)

HAMLET: 'Sblood! What's this!

HORATIA: Come away, My Lord… We must away to Norway! *(She pulls him off the stage, kicking and stamping all the way off).*

HAMLET (*As the light fades*): Drat!

(The stage is finally completely dark, and…)

THE PLAY IS OVER